Sprint It!

The Little Book of Word Sprints

Created & Designed By
TeeCee Design Studio

Date

Working Title

Current Word Count

Daily Word Goal

Sprint Length	Start Time	End Time	Final Count

Notes

Date

Working Title

Current Word Count

Daily Word Goal

Sprint Length	Start Time	End Time	Final Count

Notes

Date

Working Title

Current Word Count

Daily Word Goal

Sprint Length	Start Time	End Time	Final Count

Notes

Date

Working Title

Current Word Count

Daily Word Goal

Sprint Length	Start Time	End Time	Final Count

Notes

Date

Working Title

Current Word Count

Daily Word Goal

Sprint Length	Start Time	End Time	Final Count

Notes

Date	Working Title

Current Word Count

Daily Word Goal

Sprint Length	Start Time	End Time	Final Count

Notes

Date

Working Title

Current Word Count

Daily Word Goal

Sprint Length	Start Time	End Time	Final Count

Notes

Date		Working Title	

Current Word Count		Daily Word Goal	

Sprint Length	Start Time	End Time	Final Count

Notes

Date	Working Title

Current Word Count	Daily Word Goal

Sprint Length	Start Time	End Time	Final Count

Notes

Date

Working Title

Current Word Count

Daily Word Goal

Sprint Length	Start Time	End Time	Final Count

Notes

Date   Working Title

Date

Working Title

Current Word Count

Daily Word Goal

Sprint Length	Start Time	End Time	Final Count

Notes

Date

Working Title

Current Word Count

Daily Word Goal

Sprint Length	Start Time	End Time	Final Count

Notes

____

____

____

____

<table>
<tr><td colspan="2">Date</td><td colspan="2">Working Title</td></tr>
</table>

Date

Working Title

Current Word Count

Daily Word Goal

Sprint Length	Start Time	End Time	Final Count

Notes

Date

Working Title

Current Word Count

Daily Word Goal

Sprint Length	Start Time	End Time	Final Count

Notes

____

____

____

____

____

<table>
<tr><td>Date</td><td colspan="3">Working Title</td></tr>
</table>

Date		Working Title	

Current Word Count		Daily Word Goal	

Sprint Length	Start Time	End Time	Final Count

Notes
____
____
____
____
____

<table>
<tr><td>Date</td><td>Working Title</td></tr>
</table>

Current Word Count

Daily Word Goal

Sprint Length	Start Time	End Time	Final Count

Notes

<table>
<tr><td>Date</td><td colspan="3">Working Title</td></tr>
</table>

Current Word Count

Daily Word Goal

Sprint Length	Start Time	End Time	Final Count

Notes

____

____

____

____

Date

Working Title

Current Word Count

Daily Word Goal

Sprint Length	Start Time	End Time	Final Count

Notes

Date

Working Title

Current Word Count

Daily Word Goal

Sprint Length	Start Time	End Time	Final Count

Notes

Date

Working Title

Current Word Count

Daily Word Goal

Sprint Length	Start Time	End Time	Final Count

Notes

Date

Working Title

Current Word Count

Daily Word Goal

Sprint Length	Start Time	End Time	Final Count

Notes
____
____
____
____
____

Date

Working Title

Current Word Count

Daily Word Goal

Sprint Length	Start Time	End Time	Final Count

Notes

Date		Working Title	

Current Word Count	Daily Word Goal

Sprint Length	Start Time	End Time	Final Count

Notes

____

____

____

____

Date

Working Title

Current Word Count

Daily Word Goal

Sprint Length	Start Time	End Time	Final Count

Notes

Date

Working Title

Current Word Count

Daily Word Goal

Sprint Length	Start Time	End Time	Final Count

Notes

Date	Working Title

Current Word Count	Daily Word Goal

Sprint Length	Start Time	End Time	Final Count

Notes

____

____

____

____

Date	Working Title

Current Word Count	Daily Word Goal

Sprint Length	Start Time	End Time	Final Count

Notes

____

____

____

____

Date   Working Title

Current Word Count   Daily Word Goal

Sprint Length	Start Time	End Time	Final Count

Notes

Date

Working Title

Current Word Count

Daily Word Goal

Sprint Length	Start Time	End Time	Final Count

Notes

Date		Working Title	

Current Word Count		Daily Word Goal	

Sprint Length	Start Time	End Time	Final Count

Notes

<table>
<tr><td colspan="2">Date</td><td colspan="2">Working Title</td></tr>
<tr><td colspan="2"></td><td colspan="2"></td></tr>
</table>

Current Word Count

Daily Word Goal

Sprint Length	Start Time	End Time	Final Count

Notes
____
____
____
____

Date

Working Title

Current Word Count

Daily Word Goal

Sprint Length	Start Time	End Time	Final Count

Notes

Date

Working Title

Current Word Count

Daily Word Goal

Sprint Length	Start Time	End Time	Final Count

Notes

Date

Working Title

Current Word Count

Daily Word Goal

Sprint Length	Start Time	End Time	Final Count

Notes

Date

Working Title

Current Word Count

Daily Word Goal

Sprint Length	Start Time	End Time	Final Count

Notes

Date

Working Title

Current Word Count

Daily Word Goal

Sprint Length	Start Time	End Time	Final Count

Notes

<table>
<tr><td>Date</td><td colspan="3">Working Title</td></tr>
</table>

Current Word Count

Daily Word Goal

Sprint Length	Start Time	End Time	Final Count

Notes

Date

Working Title

Current Word Count

Daily Word Goal

Sprint Length	Start Time	End Time	Final Count

Notes

____

____

____

____

Date

Working Title

Current Word Count

Daily Word Goal

Sprint Length	Start Time	End Time	Final Count

Notes

Date		Working Title	

Current Word Count	Daily Word Goal

Sprint Length	Start Time	End Time	Final Count

Notes

Date

Working Title

Current Word Count

Daily Word Goal

Sprint Length	Start Time	End Time	Final Count

Notes

Date		Working Title	

Current Word Count	Daily Word Goal

Sprint Length	Start Time	End Time	Final Count

Notes
____

____

____

____

____

Date

Working Title

Current Word Count

Daily Word Goal

Sprint Length	Start Time	End Time	Final Count

Notes
____
____
____
____
____

Date

Working Title

Current Word Count

Daily Word Goal

Sprint Length	Start Time	End Time	Final Count

Notes

Date

Working Title

Current Word Count

Daily Word Goal

Sprint Length	Start Time	End Time	Final Count

Notes

Date

Working Title

Current Word Count

Daily Word Goal

Sprint Length	Start Time	End Time	Final Count

Notes

Date

Working Title

Current Word Count

Daily Word Goal

Sprint Length	Start Time	End Time	Final Count

Notes

Date		Working Title	

Current Word Count		Daily Word Goal	

Sprint Length	Start Time	End Time	Final Count

Notes

____

____

____

____

Date	Working Title

Current Word Count	Daily Word Goal

Sprint Length	Start Time	End Time	Final Count

Notes

____

____

____

____

Date		Working Title	

Current Word Count		Daily Word Goal	

Sprint Length	Start Time	End Time	Final Count

Notes
____
____
____
____
____

Date

Working Title

Current Word Count

Daily Word Goal

Sprint Length	Start Time	End Time	Final Count

Notes

Date

Working Title

Current Word Count

Daily Word Goal

Sprint Length	Start Time	End Time	Final Count

Notes

Date		Working Title	

Current Word Count	Daily Word Goal

Sprint Length	Start Time	End Time	Final Count

Notes
____
____
____
____

Date

Working Title

Current Word Count

Daily Word Goal

Sprint Length	Start Time	End Time	Final Count

Notes

Date

Working Title

Current Word Count

Daily Word Goal

Sprint Length	Start Time	End Time	Final Count

Notes

Date

Working Title

Current Word Count

Daily Word Goal

Sprint Length	Start Time	End Time	Final Count

Notes

____

____

____

____

____

Date

Working Title

Current Word Count

Daily Word Goal

Sprint Length	Start Time	End Time	Final Count

Notes

____

____

____

____

Date

Working Title

Current Word Count

Daily Word Goal

Sprint Length	Start Time	End Time	Final Count

Notes

<table>
<tr><td>Date</td><td colspan="3">Working Title</td></tr>
</table>

<table>
<tr><td>Current Word Count</td><td>Daily Word Goal</td></tr>
</table>

Sprint Length	Start Time	End Time	Final Count

Notes

____

____

____

____

Date		Working Title	

Current Word Count		Daily Word Goal	

Sprint Length	Start Time	End Time	Final Count

Notes

Date

Working Title

Current Word Count

Daily Word Goal

Sprint Length	Start Time	End Time	Final Count

Notes

Date

Working Title

Current Word Count

Daily Word Goal

Sprint Length	Start Time	End Time	Final Count

Notes

Date		Working Title	

Current Word Count		Daily Word Goal	

Sprint Length	Start Time	End Time	Final Count

Notes

Date		Working Title	

Current Word Count		Daily Word Goal	

Sprint Length	Start Time	End Time	Final Count

Notes

____

____

____

____

____

Date

Working Title

Current Word Count

Daily Word Goal

Sprint Length	Start Time	End Time	Final Count

Notes

Date			

Working Title

Current Word Count

Daily Word Goal

Sprint Length	Start Time	End Time	Final Count

Notes

____

____

____

____

____

Date

Working Title

Current Word Count

Daily Word Goal

Sprint Length	Start Time	End Time	Final Count

Notes

Date		Working Title	

Current Word Count		Daily Word Goal	

Sprint Length	Start Time	End Time	Final Count

Notes

____

____

____

____

____

Date

Working Title

Current Word Count

Daily Word Goal

Sprint Length	Start Time	End Time	Final Count

Notes

Date		Working Title	

Current Word Count		Daily Word Goal	

Sprint Length	Start Time	End Time	Final Count

Notes

Date

Working Title

Current Word Count

Daily Word Goal

Sprint Length	Start Time	End Time	Final Count

Notes

Date

Working Title

Current Word Count

Daily Word Goal

Sprint Length	Start Time	End Time	Final Count

Notes

Date

Working Title

Current Word Count

Daily Word Goal

Sprint Length	Start Time	End Time	Final Count

Notes

____

____

____

____

____

Date		Working Title	

Current Word Count	Daily Word Goal

Sprint Length	Start Time	End Time	Final Count

Notes

____

____

____

____

Date		Working Title	

Current Word Count		Daily Word Goal	

Sprint Length	Start Time	End Time	Final Count

Notes

Date

Working Title

Current Word Count

Daily Word Goal

Sprint Length	Start Time	End Time	Final Count

Notes

Date		Working Title	

Current Word Count			Daily Word Goal

Sprint Length	Start Time	End Time	Final Count

Notes

____

____

____

____

Date

Working Title

Current Word Count

Daily Word Goal

Sprint Length	Start Time	End Time	Final Count

Notes

Date

Working Title

Current Word Count

Daily Word Goal

Sprint Length	Start Time	End Time	Final Count

Notes

Date

Working Title

Current Word Count

Daily Word Goal

Sprint Length	Start Time	End Time	Final Count

Notes

Date

Working Title

Current Word Count

Daily Word Goal

Sprint Length	Start Time	End Time	Final Count

Notes

Date

Working Title

Current Word Count

Daily Word Goal

Sprint Length	Start Time	End Time	Final Count

Notes

<table>
<tr><td>Date</td><td colspan="3">Working Title</td></tr>
</table>

Current Word Count

Daily Word Goal

Sprint Length	Start Time	End Time	Final Count

Notes

<table>
<tr><td>Date</td><td colspan="3">Working Title</td></tr>
</table>

Current Word Count

Daily Word Goal

Sprint Length	Start Time	End Time	Final Count

Notes

Date
Working Title

Current Word Count

Daily Word Goal

Sprint Length	Start Time	End Time	Final Count

Notes

Date

Working Title

Current Word Count

Daily Word Goal

Sprint Length	Start Time	End Time	Final Count

Notes

Date	Working Title

Current Word Count	Daily Word Goal

Sprint Length	Start Time	End Time	Final Count

Notes

Date

Working Title

Current Word Count

Daily Word Goal

Sprint Length	Start Time	End Time	Final Count

Notes

Date			Working Title

Current Word Count			Daily Word Goal

Sprint Length	Start Time	End Time	Final Count

Notes
____

____

____

____

____

Date

Working Title

Current Word Count

Daily Word Goal

Sprint Length	Start Time	End Time	Final Count

Notes

Date

Working Title

Current Word Count

Daily Word Goal

Sprint Length	Start Time	End Time	Final Count

Notes

Date		Working Title	

Current Word Count		Daily Word Goal	

Sprint Length	Start Time	End Time	Final Count

Notes

Date		Working Title	

Current Word Count		Daily Word Goal	

Sprint Length	Start Time	End Time	Final Count

Notes

Date

Working Title

Current Word Count

Daily Word Goal

Sprint Length	Start Time	End Time	Final Count

Notes

Date

Working Title

Current Word Count

Daily Word Goal

Sprint Length	Start Time	End Time	Final Count

Notes

Date		Working Title	

Current Word Count		Daily Word Goal	

Sprint Length	Start Time	End Time	Final Count

Notes

____

____

____

____

Date

Working Title

Current Word Count

Daily Word Goal

Sprint Length	Start Time	End Time	Final Count

Notes

____

____

____

____

____

Date		Working Title	

Current Word Count		Daily Word Goal	

Sprint Length	Start Time	End Time	Final Count

Notes

Date

Working Title

Current Word Count

Daily Word Goal

Sprint Length	Start Time	End Time	Final Count

Notes

Date		Working Title	

Current Word Count		Daily Word Goal	

Sprint Length	Start Time	End Time	Final Count

Notes

Thank you so much for your purchase.

I really do hope that this book has helped you,
even in some small way.

Would you like to see different designs/styles?

I am always very happy to hear from customers,
so please feel free to email me on

teeceedesignstudio@yahoo.com